JANE PACKER
AT HOME WITH FLOWERS

Photography by Catherine Gratwicke

JANE PACKER
AT HOME WITH FLOWERS

Beautifully simple arrangements for every room in the house

RYLAND
PETERS
& SMALL
LONDON NEW YORK

Senior designer Sonya Nathoo
Commissioning editor Annabel Morgan
Location research Jess Walton
Production Toby Marshall
Art director Leslie Harrington
Publishing director Alison Starling

Styling Lesley Dilcock

First published in 2011
by Ryland Peters & Small
20–21 Jockey's Fields
London WC1R 4BW
and
519 Broadway, 5th Floor
New York, NY 10012
www.rylandpeters.com

10 9 8 7 6 5 4 3 2 1
Text © Jane Packer 2011
Design and photographs
© Ryland Peters & Small 2011

ISBN: 978-1-84975-119-3

A CIP record for this book is
available from the British Library.

Printed and bound in China

 For digital editions visit
www.rylandpeters.com/apps.php

Library of Congress Cataloging-in-
Publication Data

Packer, Jane, 1959-
  Jane Packer at home with flowers : beautifully
simple arrangements for every room in the
house / photography by Catherine Gratwicke. --
1st ed.
    p. cm.
  Includes index.
  ISBN 978-1-84975-119-3
  1. Flower arrangement in interior decoration.
I. Gratwicke, Catherine. II. Title. III. Title: At home
with flowers. IV. Title: Beautifully simple
arrangements for every room in the house.
  SB449.P2245 2011
  745.92--dc22
                                      2010051126

CONTENTS

INTRODUCTION

At Home with Flowers is special to me as it showcases floral arrangements that are genuinely easy to achieve yet are also creative and inspiring. My aim with this book was to enable people to put flowers together in a naturalistic and uncontrived manner. Flower arranging doesn't have to be complicated, so don't worry about following rules or needing special skills. All you need is some imagination, an eagerness to experiment and an ability to see beyond the norm. These arrangements are truly simple and straightforward. Better still, they use easily obtainable blooms and, at the same time, all the flowers retain the signature Jane Packer style that I have developed over the years.

Not everyone has a big budget for flowers and I have kept this in mind when devising the arrangements. Clever choice of containers can result in some fantastic effects and allow you to use fewer flowers. In many places I have clustered vases together and popped flowers into only a few of the containers. This creates a feeling of abundance and celebration, despite using only five or six stems. If the amount of flowers in some of the arrangements seems extravagant, save them for special occasions and remember that just a few beautiful stems arranged in the right way can also make an amazing impact on your home.

Look with fresh eyes at the containers you have at home. Beautiful flowers don't require family heirloom crystal vases. Often the unexpected – a tea caddy or an old umbrella stand – excites the most comment and admiration. Remember – fresh flowers should make you happy, and if they make you smile too, then so much the better!

This has been the hardest book I have ever worked on and the whole process has been a real battle for me. While writing the book I suffered a stroke and I have been fighting my disability ever since. For someone who has been super-fit all through her life, this was a real shock and I have needed a lot of care and attention to make this book happen. I have had so much help from my wonderful Jane Packer team and I couldn't be more grateful. I am happy to say that I am now on the mend, thanks to lots of hard work and determination.

I do hope this book fires your imagination and gives you the confidence to create.

Enjoy!

Jane Packer

BUYING, CONDITIONING AND REVIVING

If you choose flowers carefully and look after them well, they will give you pleasure for longer. This process starts in the flower shop, where following a few simple pointers should prevent you from ending up with wilted flowers that only last a day or two. Make sure that all the flowers on the stand have their stems in clean water. Avoid any flowers with soft, floppy heads or petals that are starting to brown at the edges. Stems that are shedding leaves onto the floor beneath the bucket will also be past their best. If possible, inspect the stems. Cut stems will brown at the site of the cut – an indication that they've been hanging around for a while. Look for flowers with pert heads and some stems that are still in bud. Leaves should be firm and a fresh green colour (not yellowing).

CONDITIONING CUT FLOWERS

Sometimes flowers are not given enough water, so they need a good long drink to quench their thirst. When you get them home, re-cut the stems at an angle to enlarge the surface area – this will enable more water to be taken up. Remove any foliage from the lower part of the stem, to help keep the water clean. Now plunge your flowers into a deep container of water. If there's a sachet of flower food attached to your flowers, make sure you use it. Flower food provides nutrients that encourage buds to open, and helps to keep a vase bacteria-free, prolonging the life of your flowers. Whether you have purchased a beautiful bouquet or a single rose, the rule is the same – change the water every day and your flowers will last longer.

CONDITIONING BOUQUETS

If you are lucky enough to be given a beautiful bouquet, the same rules apply. Trim the stems on the diagonal, only taking off a small amount (otherwise you may spoil the proportions), and remove any foliage below the water line. Don't cut the string holding the bouquet together, otherwise the lovely arrangement will simply fall apart.

REVIVING FLOPPY HEADS

If they go for too long out of water, many flowers will hang their heads. However, there is a way to revive them. Take several sheets of paper and lay the stems on top. Now firmly roll the paper around the flowers so that any drooping heads are held upright. Re-cut the stems at an angle and stand them in water for several hours, then unwrap. Some flowers are thirstier than others. The whole heads of hydrangea or roses can be plunged into cold water to revive them. Misting flowerheads with water will perk them up and, done every day, will also increase the longevity of your flowers.

DESIGN PHILOSOPHY

My design philosophy is very simple. My inspiration is and always has been nature – the way flowers grow on the plant. Accordingly, a 'signature' Jane Packer bouquet or arrangement is limited to one colour, sometimes in a range of tones (from lilac to deep purple, for example) and will include no more than three or four different varieties of flower. Limiting the number of varieties creates impact and allows the onlooker to appreciate the unique beauty of each one. Instead of mixing up the blooms and dotting them around the arrangement at intervals, I like to cluster each variety together for a random, naturalistic effect. I sometimes take this idea one step further by buying two or three different varieties of flower in the same shade, then arranging them separately in vases of varying shape and height. The result is simple, beautiful and elegant arrangements that never look stiff, ostentatious or contrived.

BALANCE AND HARMONY
When it comes to arranging flowers, the aim is to marry up flowers and a container to create a harmonious and balanced whole. Both should be sympathetic to each other, and neither should dominate. If I have a very decorative vase, I pair it with the simplest of flowers – a single hydrangea head, perhaps, or a couple of arum lilies. By the same token, a large, dramatic arrangement needs a container that won't compete with the flowers. The traditional rule of using an odd number of flowers in an arrangement still stands. An odd number will result in a composition that's less regimented and has the asymmetrical randomness of nature.

VASES AND CONTAINERS
If you enjoy living with flowers, it's a good idea to build up a 'library' of vases and containers in varying shapes, colours and materials to enable you to create arrangements of different sizes and styles. A tall, cylindrical vase is good for showcasing long-stemmed flowers such as amaryllis or lilies at eye level or on a mantelpiece. A low, square tank is great for coffee-table arrangements. The key is to have enough flowers to fill the vase and to cut the stems short so that the flowerheads mass densely just above the neck of the container. Other useful vases include the classic flared shape. This requires a large quantity of flowers to fill its wide mouth, so works well with more inexpensive blooms such as tulips or narcissus. And then there are dainty little bud vases that display just one perfect bloom. Nowadays, I love to cluster a number of small vases together, each holding just one or two stems. This looks fresh and modern, and gives great value for money, since you don't need as many flowers.

FAVOURITE FLOWERS

I have to confess that my favourite flowers change all the time. When you work with flowers day in day out, you get bored with things quickly. Familiarity breeds contempt, if you like, and favourite flowers soon lose their novelty value. However, some do stand the test of time. Often, breeders will put a new spin on an old favourite by offering it in a new colour. Delphiniums, for example, are now available in luscious shades of peach, as well as the classic blue and purple hues. Breeders also work to develop new varieties or forms – like bigger roses and more luscious double peonies. In addition, the wheel of fashion turns and once-popular flowers that have fallen from favour come back into vogue, to be used in fresh ways that make them relevant and exciting again.

Although nowadays you can get many flowers all year round, at Jane Packer we try to use those that are in season. There are a few wonderful 'luxury' flowers that appear for a few short weeks only every year, such as peonies or lily-of-the-valley. They can sometimes be obtained out of season, but tend to be very expensive and often the quality isn't great. Many of these flowers have a very short vase life – stocks or lily-of-the-valley, for example. Just enjoy them as a fleeting pleasure and don't expect them to last, or you'll be disappointed.

I've always loved roses. They are the signature Jane Packer flower and epitomize luxury and glamour. When I first started out in floristry, there were only four or five different roses around. Now there are literally thousands available. Roses are beloved of florists for many reasons. They are long-lasting, available in ever-bigger sizes and make a great focal point for an arrangement. The wedding market is huge and new roses are developed to meet the demand every year. The trend at the moment is for scented roses that resemble blousy garden varieties for a romantic vintage feel.

There are many robust flowers that will last a week or more. Chrysanthemums, for example, are as tough as old boots. The shaggy green variety were fashionable a few years back, but I still can't bring myself to love them. Carnations are also long-lasting and offer value for money. The flowers aren't particularly special, but the secret is to buy and arrange them en masse to make an impact.

I'm sometimes asked what my 'Desert Island' flower would be, but it changes all the time. My current favourite is alliums and their sculptural seedpods. There isn't one flower I can pick out as a favourite, but then I'm lucky – the beauty of being a florist is that I don't have to!

Overlooked and underloved, the hallway often tends to be a rather neglected area of the home. However, fresh flowers will bring your hallway to life and create a warm welcome.

HALLWAYS

Hallways often strike me as the Cinderella of the home; they are frequently unloved, neglected and decidedly scruffy, home to discarded shoes, coats, umbrellas, bicycle helmets, junk mail and 101 other household items that haven't yet found a home. I think this is a great shame. After all, the hallway is the entrance to your home and sets the scene for what is to follow, giving visitors an important first impression of your lifestyle and personal tastes. At the same time, hallways are a high traffic area, with children, family, friends, pets, delivery services and tradespeople all coming in and out. As such, they are practical spaces and need to be kept clutter-free and streamlined – something to bear in mind when you are adorning them with flowers.

For me, the entrance hall is one area of my home that cries out for fresh flowers. It's the place where I welcome my guests, and I enjoy transforming it with the use of flowers. After all, first impressions count, and you never know who is going to pop round for a visit! I love using scented blooms in the hallway to greet you with their evocative perfume when you step through the front door after a long, hard day. My favourites would have to be lavender, sweet peas, peonies, Paperwhite narcissus and hyacinths.

Halls vary greatly in shape and size, so make the most of the space you have available. A narrow, corridor-style hall is often dominated by a large staircase at one end. It is easy to complement this style of hall by placing a large vase of flowers at the foot of the stairs. Choose a tall, slender vase and fill it with structural flowers such as gladioli, arum lilies and delphiniums; elegant, tall-stemmed blooms that echo the strong verticals of the staircase.

If your hallway is wide enough to hold a narrow console table, this is the perfect platform for fresh flowers. My console is covered with an assortment of interesting vases in different colours, shapes and sizes. These vases make an attractive display when empty, but look even better when filled with flowers. I have also invested in an armful of dramatic, flocked black branches that stand in a tall black glass vase and make an unusual focal point.

If you are lucky enough to have a large entrance hall, you can really go to town with flowers. A large vase arrangement on the floor or placed to the side of a chair can make a bold statement, but don't forget that a bud vase containing a single beautiful specimen flower positioned on a side table can have just as much of an impact. If you have the space, why not opt for both?

It's lots of fun dressing the hallway for a special occasion, whether it be a wedding, homecoming or a summer party. And at Christmas time, you have every excuse to deck the halls, introducing glossy evergreen wreaths, aromatic garlands of pine and perhaps even a Christmas tree, depending on your space. However, as you might guess, I don't think you really need an excuse to introduce flowers into your home, and the entrance hall is the best chance to showcase your personality and to welcome guests with open arms.

ABOVE These lemon-yellow hydrangeas look completely natural, but are in fact dyed. Their densely petalled heads look so fabulous that I'd arrange them alone rather than mix them with other flowers.

OPPOSITE Statice is a flower that all but disappeared from smart florists due to its frumpy, old-ladyish image. However, it is becoming popular all over again, due to its longevity and huge range of colours. Statice is low-maintenance and dries well; it's guaranteed to brighten up even the darkest of hallways.

[PREVIOUS PAGES] On a narrow hall table, tall, scented sweet peas stand alongside tiny button-like zinnias, perfectly formed dahlias and blowsy peonies. Surprisingly few flowers have been used, but the cluster of vases and candles of different sizes, shapes and heights creates the impression of abundance.

LEFT White arum lilies are truly classic but have a contemporary feel, thanks to their sleek, architectural good looks. In this economical yet very effective arrangement, five long-stemmed arums have been divided up between three very similar vases of varying heights. Note how the flowers have been arranged to fall in different directions to give interest and structure to the composition. As well as having a flawless Art Deco-style elegance, arums are robust flowers and should last for at least a week in a cool area such as a hall. However, the stems are fleshy and prone to making the water murky, so it's advisable to change the water regularly – every day, if possible.

[OVERLEAF] A mass of red and green dendrobium orchids is casually arranged in a tall ceramic vase in this London entrance hall. The vivid lime-green and chilli-pepper hues make for a bold and unexpected colour combination that works surprisingly well in this vibrant and eclectic interior. Dendrobium orchids are especially long-lasting, which makes them good value for money. You'll be able to tell when they are near the end of their life, as the flowers will delicately fall from the stem.

[PREVIOUS PAGES] Once upon a time you could only obtain amaryllis during the winter months, and then only in the traditional red or white colours. Nowadays there are so many fantastic and eye-catching varieties available and the selection increases every year. Fresh amaryllis appear in the shop in tight bud, and we all wait to see them open to an astounding size in dazzling shades of orange, pink and even yellow (although these are dyed). And as well as the exciting new colourways, there are also smaller, daintier forms now available. Here, I chose a fiery tomato red variety with a pure white centre. The shapely blooms bring a touch of heat and drama to a narrow mirrored chest in a cool white entrance hall. The arrangement is very simple, but using two identical vases in different sizes doubles the impact.

OPPOSITE AND RIGHT I love the idea of decorating an existing item in your home especially for a celebration. These foliage garlands are both long-lasting and easy to make. Garland-making may seem fiddly to start with but, like anything, it becomes easy once you get the hang of it. Start with a strong piece of twine cut to your desired length. Using wire, bind small groups of foliage onto and along the twine. Soon you will have achieved a length of continuous foliage. Here, I have used senecio (left) and silver brunia (right). Other foliage types perfect for a garland are berried ivy, eucalyptus and, of course, fragrant pine. As the garland is not in water, it's essential that it's made of robust foliage that won't wilt immediately.

ABOVE I love this design – it is just so striking. The perfectly formed black corn cobs provide a stark contrast to the dried husks, which have contorted shapes that make them look almost as if they are blowing in the wind. Arranging the corns to one side of the glossy gourd-like vase allows us to appreciate the shape of the vase while giving the arrangement a very contemporary look. It's always exciting when you can find a new ingredient to play around with and produce something unexpectedly beautiful.

OPPOSITE This arrangement combines oak leaves that have been dyed vibrant purple and delicate red skimmia. The urn-shaped vase is very classic, but against a black wall the display takes on a modern feel that suits the space. I love the way the purply red of the oak and skimmia brings the entrance to life.

One of the quickest ways to make a living room feel special is to use flowers. They remind us of the natural world, the changing seasons and the planet that we live on.

LIVING ROOMS

Your living room may be large or small but, whatever its size, it should be a space that makes everyone in the family feel relaxed and comfortable. The best living rooms always appear cosy and welcoming, no matter what season it is. We often choose to accessorize with cushions, lamps or other bits and pieces, but I believe that it's flowers that truly bring a living room to life.

When it comes to choosing flowers for the living room, first consider your space. It's essential to select blooms that coordinate with the other colours in the room. Although I usually like to ring the changes, I have to admit that at home I turn to the same old favourites time and time again – dramatic, luxurious red blooms such as roses or amaryllis, largely due to the fact that they are perfectly offset by the moody grey shade of my sitting room walls.

Next, think about the opportunities for flowers within the room – would your mantelpiece be brought to life with a bowl of gardenias, or do you have bookshelves that you can decorate with a procession of pottery elephants each holding a single rose? Coffee-table arrangements are perennially popular, and make a good focal point. They are usually designed to be seen close up or from above, and as such they lend themselves to single-flower arrangements; intricate flowers such as dahlias or hydrangeas that invite close inspection due to their densely petalled heads. Large fireplaces are the place for bold floorstanding displays in statement vases that make an impact and draw all eyes. Go to town with armfuls of delphiniums or stately amaryllis. Don't neglect other areas – bookshelves, mantelpieces or side tables will all be enlivened by the addition of flowers. On a side table, use a table lamp to spotlight a bud vase holding a single perfect rose, or cluster a group of vases in the same material or colour on a console table, then fill each one with luscious pink peonies. Sitting rooms often have to play host to a work or study zone, squeezed into a small corner, but flowers can make a workspace a pleasure to spend time in. A tiny posy of sweet peas beside the computer will give you something to muse on as you file your tax return.

I love entertaining and find that one of the quickest ways to dress the living room for a party is to use seasonal flowers. In springtime, fragrant blooms add an extra dimension – think of the heady perfume of hyacinths and narcissus. Also available at this time of year are branches of blossom, pussy willow or sticky bud, all of which can create dramatic displays while offering good value for money. If you are lucky enough to have an ornamental fruit tree in your garden, snap off a couple of branches and bring them indoors for a breath of springtime. By summer, you'll be spoilt for choice. Some of my favourites are hydrangeas, peonies, garden roses, pinks and stocks, many of which also have the benefit of scent. Summer flowers – stocks, for example – are not always long-lived, but often their fast-falling petals only add to their evocative allure. By autumn, ring the changes with dramatic leaves and foliage arrangements. And in winter, go for berried branches, glossy evergreens, architectural amaryllis and ruffle-edged brassicas.

[PREVIOUS PAGES] These cornflowers are an almost unbelievably vivid, saturated shade of blue. They are not expensive flowers yet used en masse, as here, cornflowers can create an outstanding presence. The blue ribbon in the painting behind appears to flow down to the arrangement, enhancing the colour and simplicity of the design. I chose an understated vintage glass and wire container to hold these simple but striking flowers.

OPPOSITE A vaseful of the palest powder-blue delphiniums reaches for the sky, surrounded by a ruffled collar of similarly hued hydrangeas, which add volume and depth. I have not used foliage in this composition, instead allowing the flowers to speak for themselves. This decision brings a contemporary edge to an arrangement of fairly traditional flowers.

RIGHT The vibrant deep-blue hue of gentiana is its greatest asset, along with the way the trumpet-shaped flowers arc studded along the length of the stems. Gentiana are well suited to tall, narrow vases, and due to the generous number of flowers on each stem, just one or two can create a dramatic effect.

LEFT This is a spectacular display of a jumbo variety of stachys, otherwise known as lamb's ears. Soft to the touch and with a velvety texture, it's irresistably strokeable. The huge white silver birch vase gives the arrangement even more presence. I love the contrasting textures, from the rough bark to the furry stachys and the smooth, reflective surface of the mirror glass.

OPPOSITE Eucalyptus pods are pale in colour with a beautiful silvery lustre that here is complemented by the bark wrapped around each container. When kept in water, the pods will burst open to reveal fluffy, coral-like stamens that offer a startling contrast to the hard shells. When kept out of water, the eucalyptus will remain as shown and can be a permanent feature.

[OVERLEAF] Antique trophy cups in a variety of different shapes and sizes have been planted up with a range of succulent plants. Succulents only need a little water every now and then to keep them going. They tend to do crazy things and may surprise you by unexpectedly putting forth a new stem or a vibrant flower.

OPPOSITE AND RIGHT

Encased within these amazing glass cloches and large jars sit vivid green hydrangea heads. Viewing the flowers through glass makes them feel like botanic specimens and by enclosing them they become a precious item. The idea of filling an empty fireplace with flowers is one I favour tremendously. We take for granted the warm flames of a fire in winter, but when it comes to the summer months, the fireplace is a dark, empty space crying out to be filled with colour. Although the hydrangea will dry perfectly and keep its colour, I have used small mirror-glass vases within each cloche to hold the stems and keep them fresh.

[OVERLEAF: LEFT] An armful of tulips spills lavishly out of this old brass lantern. I love using unusual containers – the result is always a talking point. With tulips, you need to re-cut the stems and change the water daily, as they carry on growing in water.

[OVERLEAF: RIGHT] Lime-yellow button dahlias have been cut to different heights and used to fill a cluster of exotic brass vases on a low table. The containers are a variety of shapes and sizes, yet are unified by the dahlias. This is a great way to showcase a collection of vases.

THIS PAGE AND OPPOSITE This design is very contemporary in style, thanks to its feeling of calm simplicity and the clean, streamlined shapes of the containers. The lower vase contains smooth, perfectly formed poppy heads sitting all in a row. I love how they aren't quite sitting straight and are bouncing off each other to keep their place within the line. The taller vase holds just three vibrant green sweet williams; so delicate and fluffy, and in complete contrast to the smooth surface of the poppy heads. Although sweet williams are not uncommon flowers, they are more usually available in shades of pink and red – this zesty green variety has only recently been introduced to the market.

ABOVE These tuberoses are simply divine. Their waxy white flowers can be slow to open, but release an amazing scent when in full bloom. Here, they are in tight bud, so have a lovely green tinge. Sometimes there is nothing more inspiring than the purity of a single type of flower. I can see myself sitting at my desk gazing at this magnificent flower and receiving a waft of its heady fragrance with every turn of a page.

OPPOSITE Yellow is not one of my favourite colours, but I absolutely love the sunny hue of this eremurus. The long stems reach up to a metre in height and are covered with tiny flowers that open from bottom to top. I have also added a few stems of fennel for its amazing scent. The colours bring new life to the image on the wall and are completely inspiring – something we all need when hard at work.

LEFT I love the old-fashioned glamour of this arrangement. The gardenia is one of my all-time favourites. The scent of the flowers is amazing and fills the room, taking your breath away with its seductive quality. And surrounding the blooms is a mass of glossy foliage. Gardenia plants have a rarity value in the northern hemisphere, as they are native to a much warmer climate – seeing them growing on the streets in Japan is a sight I will never forget.

[OVERLEAF: LEFT] Dainty white pompon chrysanthemums have been cut short and arranged in a low bowl. Chrysanthemums have flowers growing on branched stems, so cutting them short creates a random layered effect that adds depth. They are available all year round, are inexpensive and have a long vase life.

[OVERLEAF: RIGHT] This huge glass fishbowl vase is filled with white hydrangea: so simple, yet so strong. It may look as if only a few stems are required, but appearances are deceptive and you will need 10 or 11 heads to fill a bowl of this size. When making this arrangement I massed the hydrangea in a rounded shape to echo the form of the vase. Passers-by are sure to stop and stare at these beautiful flowers in awe.

LEFT This old metal crown gave me the idea for a novel way of displaying roses, which are among my favourite flowers. I have used David Austin roses, which have a slight yellow tinge and the most magnificent scent, and Vendela roses with a soft pink tone. The roses have been pushed into florist's foam and placed inside the arches to resemble the cushioned velvet interior of a crown.

OPPOSITE These tiny antique silver boots are so charming that I couldn't resist dressing them up with flowers. Peeping over the top of each boot is a dainty white aster with a bright yellow centre reminiscent of a garden daisy. The asters are the perfect size, and will sit tight and keep fresh for at least a week.

[OVERLEAF] Red alert! For this arrangement, I used three different kinds of red dahlia, ranging from deepest crimson to a brighter postbox red as well as a variegated variety with intricately detailed petals that seem to have been dipped in white paint. Dahlias come in many shapes and colours during the late summer and early autumn months. The rich, lush combination here matches the interior perfectly.

LEFT The Black Baccara rose is a deep, luscious red that's almost verging on black, hence the name. I have arranged a neat posy of the roses at the neck of a tall vase. Flowing from one side is a trail of red amaranthus, stripped of its foliage to prevent the green of the leaves detracting from the magenta flowers. This is a true statement vase, and you should never be afraid of making a statement with the flowers too.

OPPOSITE Celosia is one of the most intriguing flowers I have come across. Arrange it in a low vase so that you can appreciate the fluffy texture and the intricate whorls of the flowerheads from above. Here I have used a dark crimson variety to bring drama to the monochrome scheme.

[OVERLEAF: LEFT] With their exotic, otherwordly beauty, these dark pink vanda orchids make an unusual ceramic vase into a focal point.

[OVERLEAF: RIGHT] These densely petalled, rich red garden roses have been casually arranged to suit a relaxed modern interior.

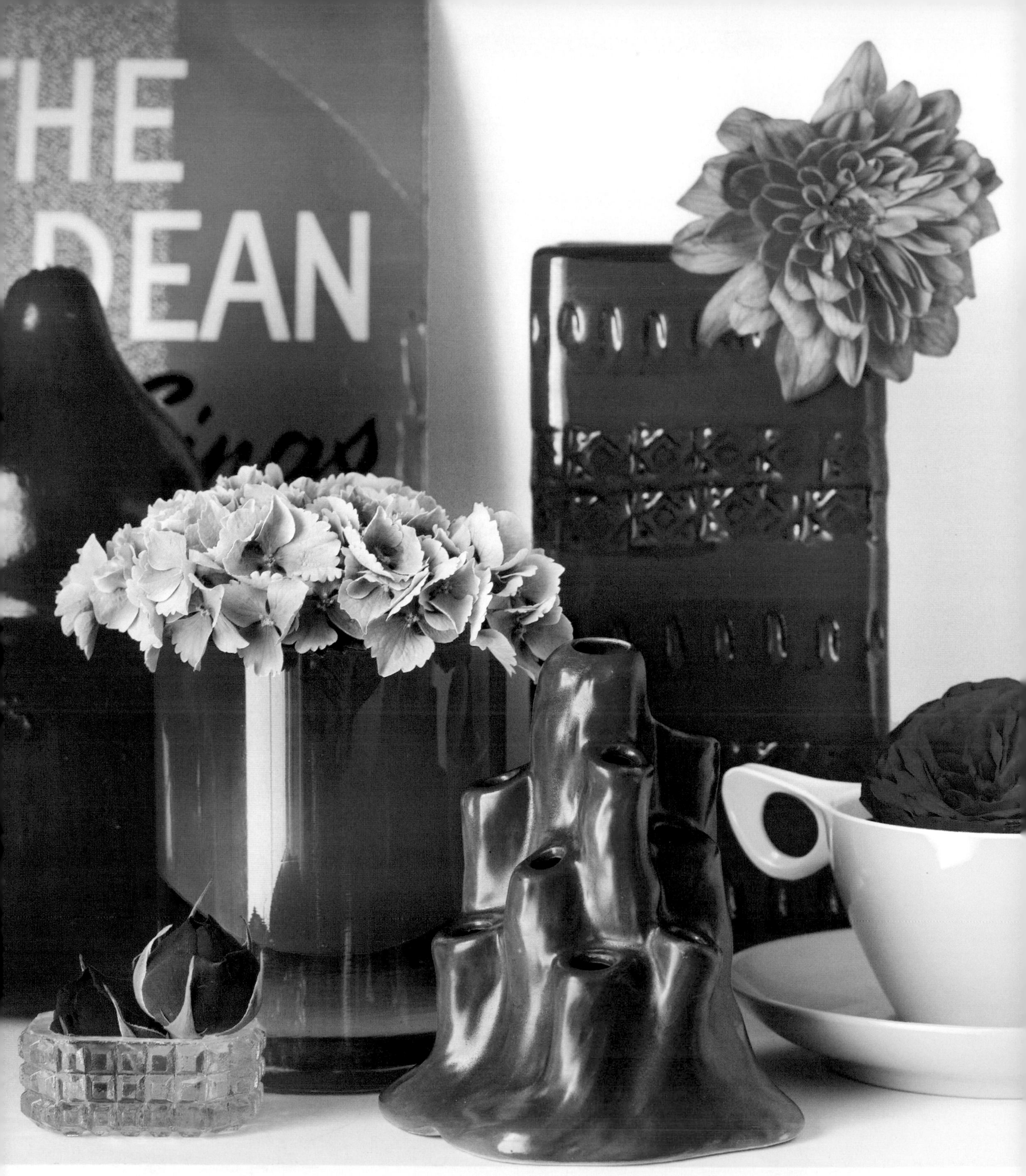
DEAN

OPPOSITE An eclectic collection of vases and containers is brought to life with the addition of a few carefully placed blooms. The flowers used are bright in colour – lime-green hydrangea, deep red roses, and a single zesty orange dahlia. The containers vary widely in terms of colour, size and shape, and include a sunny yellow 1960s-style teacup and saucer, a retro-style royal-blue vase and a tiny lime-green glass dish as well as several strong red vases. The vases and flowers shouldn't really work together, but somehow they gel, perhaps due to the vivid colours and simple shapes of the arrangement.

BELOW These elephant containers are brilliant! The smaller of the two holds three classic red roses – a total contrast to the wild eucalyptus with its fine foliage and amazing bright red seedpods.

[OVERLEAF] I absolutely love this image for its striking symmetry and use of colour. Glorious bright orange dahlias have been tied into a perfectly domed posy and popped into a retro leopard-print vase. The arrangement is a true scene-stealer, sitting proudly between two 1930s-style chairs that remind me of old-fashioned cinema seats. I can't think of anything more perfect for this prime window location.

THIS PAGE AND OPPOSITE Chocolate cosmos are one of my all-time favourite flowers. They are such a luscious deep red that they almost appear black, but they are known as chocolate cosmos not only for their colour but also for their scent. These delicate flowers are not long-lasting and have a very limited availability, but for me their rarity and fragility makes them even more special. There's no foliage or fuss with this arrangement; by displaying them in a simple black glass vase my aim is to allow the flowers to enjoy the attention they deserve.

THIS PAGE AND OPPOSITE
These amazing architectural flowers are actually globe artichokes – yes, the ones that you can eat! Although artichokes are not something you might expect to see out of the kitchen, keeping the stems long and arranging them as flowers allows us to appreciate their dramatic sculptural forms and the mesmerizing purple centres. The heads are extremely heavy and are best contained within a vase with a narrow neck and heavy base so that they are well supported.

OPPOSITE I love these monochrome containers, which combine a 1970s vibe with contemporary styling. The arum lilies are such a deep purple they are almost black and have a minimal modern feel. The arrangements prove that you don't need to completely fill a vase with flowers; creating a structure within the vase can be just as effective, if not more so.

RIGHT Feast your eyes upon the amazing hues in this small head of hydrangea – they are guaranteed to inspire a gasp of awe. Each predominantly purple petal has an electric-blue centre and veining that blends to the edges, leaving a dreamy trail of vibrant blue, pink and red. Hydrangeas are, of course, much more beautiful than pens and pencils, which is why I have placed this one in a cute black-and-white pottery pen pot – the perfect container for such an amazing flower.

THIS PAGE A few stems of the palest pink snowberry, Sweet Avalanche roses and sage-green berried eucalyptus have been dotted sparingly among this collection of pastel-hued vases. There is minimal use of flowers here – just a few stems in total – because I wanted to make a feature of the vases rather than the flowers. I think the end result is amazing. The visual effect is very strong, yet there are just three different pastel tones used in both the vases and flowers.

[OVERLEAF] It amazes me that there are new flowers being bred all the time, making it easier to keep up with colour trends in fashion and interiors. This coral-coloured delphinium is a perfect example. It is a fairly new variety and its colour is rarely found in flowers. This arrangement also demonstrates the versatility of the colour black. I could have easily used a pastel-coloured vase, yet the black shows how combining light and dark can have a fabulous outcome... sometimes!

The kitchen may not seem like the obvious place to have flowers, but what could be better than filling this area with things you love and that make you happy?

KITCHENS AND DINING SPACES

Because it's warm, homely and the place where I feel most relaxed, the kitchen is probably my favourite room in the house. Cooking is one of the great loves of my life; sitting down together to share a meal brings everyone together and welcomes so many different faces into our home. You don't need tons of flowers to dress a kitchen, and you certainly don't need show-stopping arrangements. Instead, fill the kitchen with simple, unpretentious flowers that you will enjoy every day.

The best thing about flowers in the kitchen is that they can be relaxed and informal; this is not a traditional spot for floral displays, so no-one has any expectations. This gives you lots of leeway to play around with fruit and berries as well as flowers – think rosehips and chilli peppers, or a huge bowl of artichokes with their intriguing furry textures. You don't need to buy flowers – if you have a garden, bring in flowers, foliage or blossom-strewn boughs. Trailing lengths of ivy can be used to decorate a long table, while branches of apple blossom look striking in a tall vase.

In the kitchen, it's fun to use containers that give a nod and a wink to their surroundings. Search your cupboards for quirky kitchenware such as tea caddies or coffee pots, or wash out and reuse glass food jars or milk bottles. Enamelled jugs are the perfect home for a sheaf of tulips, and you can pop a dome-shaped posy of sweet williams into a colourful glass sundae dish. Vintage coffee cans are the ideal receptacles for sooty-eyed anemones or a single luscious camelia. Even jelly moulds or copper pans can be used as vases and filled with a mass of small-headed roses. If you're arranging flowers and end up with a broken-off bloom, pop it in a shot glass, place it by the sink and contemplate its beauty while you wash the dishes.

The obvious place for kitchen flowers is the table. Keep it simple. A long table allows you to have a row of small arrangements dotted along its length. A round table is well suited to a central arrangement, but remember not to make it too tall, or it will interrupt the flow of suppertime chat. Sideboards and dressers can also play host to flowers. Place smaller arrangements where they can be enjoyed at close quarters – on a shelf, perhaps, or on the worktop alongside a pile of cookery books and the wine rack.

A separate dining room is less common nowadays, but if you do have one, the dining table calls out for flowers. They will bring the room and the table to life, and delight your guests. However, the days of stiff centrepieces built on florist's foam are long gone. Keep the flowers informal and modern, interspersed with twinkling candles. If you have a long table, it's nice to have flowers at intervals along its length. Perhaps use three identical vases each holding a low bunch of different white flowers. Alternatively, go for a mismatched row of glass bottles and jars all holding single stems of the same flower. But avoid strongly scented flowers on the dining table – any chef will tell you that they can be offputting when food is being served.

THIS PAGE Golden celosia, fiery leucospermum and lipstick-pink gloriosa lilies make for a table centrepiece that's perfect for a summer party.

OPPOSITE Red proteas and dendrobium orchids bring a dark corner to life. I couldn't resist using these fun 1970s-style ceramic carafes as vases.

OPPOSITE Like flowers, fruits have their seasons, and when pomegranates are around, I love to use and display them as often as possible. The deep crimson of their skin is so special, suitably matched by their blood-red jewel-like seeds. Here, a heap of pomegranates completely fills an oversized wooden bowl and shows that successful arrangements don't always need flowers, just a readiness to experiment with colour and texture.

RIGHT These amazing woody stems of malus apples are slightly magnified by the tall glass vase that holds them. Tiny ornamental red apples travel up the length of each stem in perfect clusters. Although the arrangement is in the kitchen, placing the apples in a vase makes it quite clear that they are intended for decoration rather than consumption! Although apples on the stem can be expensive, they will last for a few weeks and are the perfect way to herald the arrival of autumn.

RIGHT I hate to see an empty kitchen table – to my mind it cries out for friends, family, plenty of food and drink, and flowers too, of course! In this cosy family kitchen, different shades and textures of red and white bring life and interest to the kitchen table and echo the cheerful gingham cloth. Small jugs and a large decorative food tin hold a variety of blooms, including an enormous fluffy protea head dyed a vibrant red, a cluster of delicate crimson nerines, glossy rosehips and tall stems of shiny red chilli peppers.

[OVERLEAF] Everyone who sees these unopened allium seedpods is entranced by their sculptural good looks. The acid lime colour is so dramatic and striking against the kitchen blackboard, and the sleek stems, bulbous pods and smooth, almost rubbery surfaces throw into relief the rough wood of the chopping board, the sleek stainless steel and the textural ridged vases. Alliums are members of the onion family, which makes them a perfect choice for the kitchen.

ABOVE Although the delicate fronds of dill and the unripe blackberry stems displayed on this shelf are not intended for consumption, they don't look out of place in a kitchen.

OPPOSITE A wire basket full of artichokes invites us to appreciate the intriguing forms and delicate greeny-purple hues of the vegetable. As is often the case with flower arranging, using an abundance of a humble ingredient often creates more impact than a small posy of expensive stems.

[OVERLEAF] Shades of white: silver-backed senecio leaves from the garden are combined with spires of veronica, creamy white astilbe and daisy-like white astrantia, and used to adorn a collection of vintage milk bottles. These summer flowers work so well together and against the white-painted dresser.

BELOW Pompon chrysanthemums have been tucked into a vintage enamel coffee caddy found in a junk store. The way in which the flowers have been tightly grouped together is quite a modern concept, yet the container is of times past, showing how a mix of old and new can work brilliantly together.

[OVERLEAF] This little colony of comical penguin jugs is just the thing to amuse and bring fun to the kitchen – they look as if they're gathering round for a chat. I have filled the penguins with plants that will last and last in a hot, steamy kitchen environment, as they live on the moisture in the air.

THIS PAGE This is such a playful use of a vintage coffee set. I love the echinops heads piled high in the sugar bowl – they look so cute, but are not quite as sweet as sugar, since they are quite prickly to touch! The white thistle is just peeping out of the top of the pot like steam rising from hot coffee. Quirky ideas like these are a good use of flowers that wouldn't quite fit into a larger arrangement or blooms that have outlived other flowers in an arrangement.

THIS PAGE AND OPPOSITE
These pure white 'Mont Blanc'
amaryllis are absolutely
stunning with their almost
luminous, glowing green
centres. Here, I have arranged
the amaryllis in two layers to
give a contemporary feel that
suits the surroundings. The
structure of the arrangement
also allows us to appreciate the
smooth green stems and the full
large white flowers. It's such an
easy design to copy, yet the
finished result is a real attention
grabber and would definitely
have your guests talking.

ABOVE This arrangement is really quite traditional in terms of the container and the composition, but I have brought it up to date by massing the flowers together into a compact dome shape. I've combined large, full-headed white roses with smaller-budded white spray roses, bright royal-blue hyacinths and delicate astrantia. There are a lot of luxury flowers in this arrangement, so it would be quite costly. I would suggest it is used for a special occasion as a feature centrepiece on a beautifully laid table .

OPPOSITE Scabiosa were once my very favourite flower – I just couldn't believe the detail of each fragile flowerhead. This was back at the very beginning of my career when there wasn't as big a choice of flowers as there is now. Even now, when I see the first scabiosa of the season I can't help but smile. I am reminded of my past love for them and I always take a bunch home where I can admire them all day.

[PREVIOUS PAGES] A mass of summer flowers in blues, purples and cerise fills the centre of this table perfectly. This is a classic composition of scented delphiniums, stocks, peonies and roses; all my favourite things from an old-fashioned country garden. The arrangement has been made with florist's foam to hold the flowers in position and ensure a long life, and will need to be watered daily to keep both flowers and foam moist. The display would be ideal for a summer party; just add food, wine and guests!

THIS PAGE AND OPPOSITE
All the colours of the rainbow appear here, and in such bright, sunny tones too. Each vase contains a tight posy made up from a combination of different flowers that are all the same colour and hue. There's sherbet-yellow hydrangeas and dahlias, raspberry-pink dahlias, hydrangeas and asclepias, juicy orange spray roses and asclepias, deep magenta asclepias, celosia and stocks and, last but not least, perfect purple dahlias, hydrangea, scented stocks and statice.

ABOVE King proteas of the palest marshmallow pink stand tall in a glass vase that mimics a plastic water bottle. Proteas are tough flowers, as they grow in enormous heat, so they last for a few weeks. The inside of the flower has the softest texture with an almost velvety feel. Due to the size and weight of their heads, proteas must be displayed in a heavy-bottomed vase to prevent it tipping over.

OPPOSITE Here, in quite tight bud, is a jugful of wonderful purply pink-hued double tulips. Tulips fascinate me, as they continue to grow in water and thus change shape, size and colour in the vase. These tulips are quite dark now, but once open they will fade to palest lilac. Tulips are thirsty, so you'll need to keep the vase topped up with water and to re-cut the stems to keep the arrangement's shape.

OPPOSITE Stems of perfect white peppercorns tumble over the edge of an urn-shaped vase and wander in all directions. Seen against the smooth white ceramics, the peppercorns don't appear white at all, but a rich sepia tint. This is a really painterly arrangement – I think it looks like a still-life.

BELOW This design has a wintery feel and wouldn't look out of place as part of your Christmas decorations. I love the silvery grey tone of the Spanish moss surrounding the candle. So invitingly tactile and soft to the touch, it is also easily manipulated to form many shapes. The silver mesh baubles laid on top of the moss add a hint of shimmer and glamour to it and bring out its silver and grey tones.

[OVERLEAF] This mismatched gold lustre tea set looks amazing on a simple stone garden table. Like many people, I have cupboardfuls of cherished china that I do sometimes remember to bring out on special occasions, but which more often languishes behind closed doors. It is obvious I should display it more frequently, as such beautiful items deserve to be admired. The pale pink roses used here have an old-fashioned vintage feel, giving them a similar, precious quality to their container. They will last for a fairly long time and open to a huge, lavish size with different depths of nude colouring.

Waking up to fresh flowers is a real joy, so indulge yourself. Floral arrangements aren't just for show and have just as much of a place in the more private corners of the home.

BEDROOMS AND BATHROOMS

We're used to having floral arrangements in our halls and living rooms, but people don't always think of putting flowers in the bedroom. I think it's a great shame, as even the tiniest posy of fresh flowers on the bedside table or dressing table allows you to revel in the beauty of flowers close up. You can have some fun with containers too. For this more private area of the home, I love dainty vases in sugared-almond pastels or vintage-style pressed glass – after all, one woman's kitsch is another woman's treasure!

I believe that bedroom flowers should be glamorous and indulgent, and my choice of blooms in this section reflects that. Allow your yearnings for romantic, feminine blooms free rein, and choose luscious roses, feathery astilbe, ranunculus, sweet williams or lily-of-the-valley. Enjoy a bowlful of blowsy garden roses on your dressing table or a tiny vase of delicate jewel-like muscari on a bedside table. And don't forget the subtle charms of old-fashioned favourites such as sweet peas and violets. When we have people to stay overnight, I love arranging flowers for the guest bedroom – it looks so inviting and creates a hospitable effect. Arrangements don't need to be big to look effective. Matching displays on bedside tables look particularly appealing, even if they're just a single hydrangea head in a colourful glass tumbler. Add a stack of glossy magazines, bottled water and a couple of glasses for a luxurious boutique-hotel effect. If feminine flowers aren't your style, or if you are entertaining male houseguests, opt for orchids – they are sculptural and elegant without being too girly or boudoirish. Alternatively, dense, furry, many-petalled proteas are amongst my current favourites and make dramatic and unusual additions to any scheme.

I always think that bathrooms offer the perfect opportunity to use strongly scented flowers, such as hyacinths or narcissus. In a guest bathroom, pair them with scented candles to create a luxurious spa effect that will make your guests feel indulged and pampered. I also like using exotic flowers in the bathroom, as their strong, clear colours pop against white sanitaryware or tiles – think of gloriosa lilies, a sheaf of gladioli or orange kangaroo paw.

Bathrooms are also a good environment for potted plants. Choose those that love humidity, such as orchids. If you revel in heady scents, opt for gardenias or stephanotis, which will thrive in warm, humid conditions. And then there's a huge array of decorative succulents that would also do well, such as crassula, the rosette-like sempervivum or echeveria. If you struggle to keep your houseplants happy, it's worth moving them to the bathroom – you may find that they flourish in the moist conditions.

If you're having a party, flowers shouldn't be restricted to the hallway and living room. Remember a posy for the downstairs bathroom – again, scented flowers would be nice, but just a single stem in a bud vase is enough. Add a thick pile of hand towels and a scented candle as a finishing touch.

ABOVE AND OPPOSITE I love adding feminine elements to a bedroom and these two arrangements – one of veronica (above) and the other ranunculus (opposite) are perfect examples of this. Veronica – so graceful and pretty – is perfect if you want something inexpensive and long-lasting. And spring ranunculus are one of my favourites, due to the wealth of detail in their densely ruffled heads of paper-thin petals.

[OVERLEAF: LEFT] Feathery astilbe looks so delicate, but is actually quite robust and will last over a week. Here, I have used it en masse, leaving the foliage on the stems to add volume to the arrangement. It's a good choice for a bedroom, as it is odourless, so there's no heavy scent to fill the room or disturb your sleep.

[OVERLEAF: RIGHT] These phytolacca berries are amazing – there's no other word for it. Just look at the bright lipstick-pink stem travelling through the mass of glossy lime-green berries; the colours and textures are intriguing and irresistible. Phytolacca berries are highly toxic when raw, so this is an arrangement that should be avoided if you have inquisitive children or pets who might find the exotic colouring hard to resist.

OPPOSITE You might expect to find delphiniums in all shades of blue, but these dreamy lilac spires are something of a departure from the norm; the flowers range from regal purple to palest lavender. In recent years, breeders have developed delphiniums in many exciting new colours, flower forms and growing heights, and this particular delphinium is a double variety, meaning the flowers have twice as many petals as usual, which creates a wonderfully lush, bountiful effect. You don't need to do much to delphiniums – their loose, country-garden style is suited to simple arrangements. Here, I have kept the stems all the same height to give a neat finish to the arrangement.

RIGHT I have enjoyed playing around with textures here – the velvety fluffiness of the protea heads contrasts beautifully with the silky shine of the tall foliage and the glossy sheen of the bulbous black vase. The overall effect is strong and contemporary, yet when the arrangement is set alongside a collection of vintage treasures from a bygone era, the old and new work perfectly together.

THIS PAGE AND OPPOSITE I absolutely love this lavish arrangement of zesty lime-green summer flowers. The flowers are arranged in layers, with the top layer consisting of molucella, an old favourite of mine. The middle layer is a mass of guelder rose; a beautiful garden shrub with a woody stem and a pompom-like head made up of clusters of tiny green florets. Finally, tucked in around the base is a wide collar of 'Limelight' hydrangeas – a fairly new variety with a pointed conical shape and a froth of fine petals.

[OVERLEAF] This tall arrangement is a striking addition to a minimal modern bedroom. The twiggy lilac branches are so architectural and naturally beautiful that they could make a permanent decorative feature in any room; a feature that can be easily adapted with the addition of just a few flowers. I have added two stems of the most amazing phalaeonopsis orchids, sometimes known as moth orchids. Here, the waxy white flowers really do look a little like a cloud of moths or butterflies fluttering away from the branches.

THIS PAGE AND OPPOSITE
This retro-style rectangular vase is a strong turquoise shade – a colour that can be hard to match with flowers. Instead of trying to find blooms to harmonize with the vase, I've opted for eclectic-looking flowers in strong, clashing hues. Amber-yellow leucospermum nutans, with their spiky petals, are the main focus here. Leucospermum are also known as the nodding pincushion, and when you inspect them close up you can see why. I have combined these exotic blooms with sunny yellow chrysanthemums, dark-berried eucalyptus, pale pink veronica and hot pink gomphrena. The graphic design of the bedlinen enhances the riot of colours and shapes, accessorizing the flowers still further.

THIS PAGE This white china toothbrush holder has been put to a new use as a vase for single stems. The toothbrushes have been replaced by vibrant orange asclepias, which fit perfectly in each hole. I love the zing of colour they add to a pure white space.

OPPOSITE It seemed right to add a touch of bold colour to the warm, neutral tones of this bathroom. I chose three vases in similarly subdued, warm tones and with organic shapes that echo the pebbles on the floor. The larger vase holds a large bundle of fiery orange crocosmia, while just three heads of orange and yellow leucospermum nutans seem to pop like firecrackers out of the smallest fishbowl vase.

OPPOSITE Cut from the garden, these spires of white lysimachia seemed to me to mirror a swan's white plumage. I love the way they randomly but gracefully twist and turn as they grow. This rather kitsch arrangement seems to come to life floating across the white ceramic floor tiles, the eccentric personality of the swan entirely in tune with the quirky patchwork armchair. I think every vase collection needs a few weird and wonderful containers like this one.

BELOW This old-fashioned ceramic shell has been filled with heads of white sedum, still so tightly in bud that you can only just about make out what the plant is. Just a few very short stems have been used here, but they fill the shell perfectly, as they have been tucked in so tightly. Sedum is very long-lasting and another plant that's often found in the garden. It should last a few weeks even in a hot, steamy bathroom.

ABOVE You don't need red roses in a boudoir. Here, a few red skimmia cuttings fill a tiny pearlized pink vase and sit proudly beside a kitsch pink ceramic bambi that takes me straight back to my childhood. Skimmia is the simplest of flowers, with small, berry-like buds that stay just as they are and last for quite some time. It is also available in a bright lime-green hue, but I just couldn't resist the pale red shade here.

OPPOSITE Such a large and sumptuous arrangement, but in this elegant open-plan bathroom and bedroom it doesn't look remotely out of place. A simple blue-grey ceramic vase has been filled with the aptly named 'Green Goddess' calla lilies, which open to an amazing size and will last for over a week. Surrounding the callas is a mass of white snowberry foliage, studded with pure white berries that live up to their name. A true vision of elegance and abundance that proves large arrangements aren't only for the living room.

THIS PAGE AND OPPOSITE

This emerald-green bathroom is home to a wide range of succulent plants, ranging from tiny aloe vera to large, round-leafed crassulas (often known as money plants). The plants are housed within a variety of containers made from rubber, metal and ceramics, all of which share the same natural, elemental tones. Succulents are ideal plants to be kept in a bathroom, as they can live off the moisture in the air and will need very little watering. In fact, they may even thrive under a regime of benign neglect! One succulent plant may not excite the eye, but they look jungly and dramatic when gathered together en masse, so go to town and make a feature of them.

OPPOSITE Heavenly scented white stocks are so special. These traditional cut flowers were once only available during the summer months, but nowadays the march of progress means they are readily available all year round and in so many wonderful shades too, ranging from the deepest purple to the palest pink. In this simple bathroom, I couldn't resist keeping everything snowy white. An armful of stocks has been arranged in an old galvanized metal milk churn that has a utilitarian feel, and is simple yet stunning in its timeless design. I can easily imagine relaxing in a foam-filled bath with the wonderful sweet and spicy scent of the stocks filling the room.

THIS PAGE Spring-flowering Paperwhite narcissus are another example of a perfectly scented flower for the bathroom. They are so pure in colour and simple in design, yet exude a powerful and delicious perfume that is out of all proportion to their tiny size. These delicate flowers never fail to brighten the dark days of late winter and early spring, and for that I love them.

UK SOURCES

Alfies Antiques Market
13–25 Church Street
London NW8 8DT
020 7723 6066
www.alfiesantiques.com
Huge and eclectic range of collectables, including unique vintage glassware and ceramics.

Atelier Abigail Ahern
137 Upper Street
London N1 1QP
Or shop online at
www.atelierabigailahern.com
An eclectic yet sophisticated collection of furniture and decorative objects, including vases by American designer Jonathan Adler.

Bodie and Fou
www.bodieandfou.com
Fun and imaginative containers, including rubber vases and a white ceramic 'wise owl' vase.

Bodo Sperlein
Unit 1.05 OXO Tower Wharf
Barge House Street
London SE1 9PH
(By appointment only)
020 7633 9413
www.bodosperlein.com
Ethereal, magical ceramics.

Brissi
196 Westbourne Grove
London W11 2RH
020 7727 2159
Visit www.brissi.co.uk for details of their other stores.
Pretty glass and glazed ceramic vases.

The Conran Shop
Michelin House
81 Fulham Road
London SW3 6RD
020 7589 7401
www.conran.co.uk
Cutting-edge designs, including clear glass vases in different shapes and sizes, as well as quirky Perspex containers and chunky ceramics.

Debenhams
www.debenhams.com
Carries my own Jane Packer line of vases, part of the Designers at Debenhams range.

Design Nation
020 7320 2895
www.designnation.co.uk
This website promotes British design and showcases the work of young ceramicists and glass designers.

Designers Guild
267–277 Kings Road
London SW3 5EN
020 7351 5775
www.designersguild.com
Decorative vases, some hand-crafted ceramics and tableware.

Graham & Green
4 Elgin Crescent
London W11 2HX
020 7243 8908
Visit www.grahamandgreen.co.uk to buy online or for details of their other stores.
Vases and containers in a variety of styles, from vintage chic to sleek contemporary styling.

Habitat
196–199 Tottenham Court Road
London W1T 7LG
Call 08444 991122 or visit www.habitat.co.uk for details of your nearest store.
Good-value, trend-led vases.

Heal's
196 Tottenham Court Road
London W1T 7LQ
020 7636 1666
Visit www.heals.co.uk for details of your nearest store.
Classic and contemporary styles.

Ikea
Visit www.ikea.com for details of your nearest store.
Cheap-and-cheerful vases, some of which look almost as good as their designer counterparts.

Jane Packer Flowers
32–34 New Cavendish Street
London W1G 8UE
020 7935 0787
www.jane-packer.co.uk
As well as selling glorious flowers and ready-made bouquets, the Jane Packer shop also stocks a carefully chosen selection of interesting and unusual vases and containers. This includes items from the new Jane Packer ceramics range, which reflects Jane's personal taste and unique take on flower arranging. The shop also stocks the entire Jane Packer fragrance collection, which includes scented candles.

John Lewis
300 Oxford Street
London W1A 1EX
020 7629 7711
Visit www.johnlewis.com for details of your nearest store.
A good range of affordable glass and ceramic vases, glassware and other containers.

Liberty
Regent Street
London W1B 5AH
020 7734 1234
www.liberty.co.uk
Beautiful hand-crafted pieces.

Nicole Farhi Home
17 Clifford Street
London W1S 3RG
020 7494 9051
www.nicolefarhi.com
Subtle, elegant ceramics.

Scabetti
www.scabetti.co.uk
Unusual designs by Dominic and Frances Bromley.

Selfridges & Co
400 Oxford Street
London
W1A 1AB
Good selection of glass vases, from vintage milk bottles to Dartington art glass.

Skandium
86 Marylebone High Street
London W1U 4QS
020 7935 2077
www.skandium.com
Vases by celebrated Scandinavian manufacturers, all displaying the clean-lined Scandi aesthetic.

US SOURCES

Vessel
114 Kensington Park Road
London W11 2PW
020 7727 8001
www.vesselgallery.com
*The very best contemporary glass
and ceramic design, with a strong
emphasis on Scandinavian and
Italian 20th-century glassware
and ceramics.*

Vivienne Foley
www.viviennefoley.com
*Thoughtful, beautiful pieces in
organic shapes.*

The White Company
Visit www.thewhitecompany.com
to buy online or for details of
your nearest store.
*Clear glass vases and
elegant ceramics.*

Zara Home
020 7590 6990
www.zarahome.com
*Good-value vases and containers
whose eclectic good looks belie
the very reasonable prices.*

ABC Carpet & Home
888 & 881 Broadway
New York, NY 10003
212 473 3000
Visit www.abchome.com
for details of a retail outlet
near you.
*Unusual pieces, including
collaged earthenware vases
and antique silver over copper
'birch bark' vases.*

Jonathan Adler
47 Greene Street
New York, NY 10013
212 941 8950
Visit www.jonathanadler.com for
details of their other stores.
*Groovy retro-modern vases and
tabletop accessories.*

Anthropologie
Visit www.anthropologie.com
to find a store near you.
*Quirky, well-priced vintage-
inspired vases and containers.*

Brimfield Antiques Show
Route 20
Brimfield, MA 01010
www.brimfieldshow.com
*This famous flea market runs for
a week in May, July and
September.*

The Conran Shop
888 Broadway@ABC Home
New York NY 10003
866 755 9079
www.conranusa.com
*Alvar Aalto vases and Tsé & Tsé's
test-tube inspired Vase d'Avril
as well as other retro-style
pieces in glass and ceramics.*

Crate & Barrel
Visit www.crateandbarrel.com to
find a store near you.
Good basics for a 'vase library'.

English Country Antiques
Snake Hollow Road
P.O. Box 1995
Bridgehampton, NY 11932
631 537 0606
*Period country furniture and
decorative accessories.*

Fishs Eddy
889 Broadway
New York, NY 10003
212 420 9020
Call 1 877 347 4733 or visit
www.fishseddy.com for their
other two store locations.
*Pressed glass pitchers in jewel
shades and cute toile d'Jouy
printed vintage-style ceramics.*

Gump's
135 Post Street
San Francisco, CA 94108
1 800 766 7628
www.gumps.com
*Heirloom-quality vases, bowls
and vessels.*

IKEA
Call 1 800 434 4532 or visit
www.ikea.com to find a store
near you.
*Cheap-and-cheerful glass,
ceramic and rattan vases.*

Macys
Visit www.macys.com to find a
store near you.
*Chic crystal vases from Kate
Spade, Orrefors and Vera Wang.*

Mikasa
www.mikasa.com
*Classic crystal and stoneware
vases plus art glass bud vases.*

Moss
150 Greene Street
New York, NY 10012
866 888 6677
www.mossonline.com
*Imaginative, unusual containers
in every size, shape and material
imaginable – wood, bronze, glass
and more. Also clear fishbowl
vases in a variety of colours.*

Pier One Imports
Call 212 206 1911 or visit
www.pier1.com to find a store
near you.
*Seasonal selection of affordable,
trend-led vases.*

Pottery Barn
Visit www.potterybarn.com
to find a store near you.
*Good-quality, good-value
containers, including vintage-
style mercury glass vases and
antiqued copper pitchers.*

Ruby Beets Antiques
25 Washington Street
P.O. Box 1174
Sag Harbor, NY 11963
631 899 3275
www.rubybeets.com
*Holmegaard glass, Italian pewter
bowls and Chinese porcelain.*

Target Stores
Visit www.target.com to
find a store near you.
*Clear glass vases in every size
and shape imaginable.*

INDEX

Figures in italics indicate captions.

A
alliums 13, *86*
aloe vera *135*
amaranthus *60*
amaryllis 10, *29*, 33, 34
  'Mont Blanc' *98*
anemones 80
apple blossom 79
apples, malus *85*
artichokes *70*, 79, *91*
arum lilies 10, 16, *23*, *73*
asclepias *105*, *129*
asters *56*
astrantia *91*, *100*

B
balance 10
baskets, wire *91*
bathrooms 114, *129*, *130*, *132*, *135*, *136*
bedrooms 113–14, *116*
blackberry stems *91*
blossoms 34
  apple 79
boots, silver *56*
bottles
  glass 80
  milk 80, *91*
bouquets, conditioning 9
bowls 79, *85*, 113
  sugar *95*
brassicas 34

C
calla lilies *132*
camelias 80
candles *21*, 80, 114
carnations 13
celosia *60*, *82*, *105*
centrepieces 80, *82*, 100
chairs, retro-style *65*
chilli peppers 79, *86*
china *109*

chocolate cosmos *68*
choosing flowers 9
Christmas decorations *108*
Christmas trees 16
chrysanthemums 13, *53*, *94*, *126*
cloches, glass *45*
coffee caddies *94*
coffee cans 80
coffee pots 80
coffee sets *95*
conditioning 9
containers 10, *109*
  bark-wrapped *40*
  ceramic *135*
  elephant *65*
  glass and wire *39*
  metal *135*
  monochrome *73*
  pen pot *73*
  rubber *135*
corn cobs *30*
cornflowers *39*
crassulas (money plants) 114, *135*
crocosmia *129*
crown, metal *56*
cut flowers, conditioning 9

D
dahlias *21*, 34, *45*, *56*, *65*, *105*
delphiniums 13, 16, 34, *39*, *75*, *105*, *121*
dill *91*
dishes *65*
  sundae 80
dressers 80, *91*

E
echeveria 114
eremurus *51*
eucalyptus *29*, *40*, *65*, *75*, *126*
evergreens 34

F
favourite flowers 13
feathery astilbe 113, *116*
fennel *51*
fireplaces 34, *45*
floppy heads, reviving 9

florist's foam 80, *105*
flower food 9
flowerheads
  misting 9
  reviving floppy 9
food tins *86*
fruit trees 34

G
gardenias 33, *53*, 114
garlands 16
  making *29*
gentiana *39*
gladioli 16, 114
glass cloches *45*
globe artichokes *70*
gloriosa lilies *82*, 114
gomphrena *126*
guelder roses *122*
guest bedrooms 113

H
hallways 14–31
harmony 10
houseplants 114
husks, dried *30*
hyacinths 14, *100*, 114
hydrangeas 9, 10, *21*, 34, *45*, *53*, *65*, *105*, 113–14
  'Limelight' *122*

I
ivy *29*, 79

J
jars, glass food 80
jelly moulds 80
jugs 80, *86*, *94*

K
kitchens and dining spaces 78–111

L
lanterns *45*
lavender 14
leucospermum nutans *126*, *129*
lilac branches *122*

lilies 10
  arum 10, 16, *23*, *73*
  calla *132*
  gloriosa *82*, 114
lilies of the valley 13, 113
living rooms 32–77
lysimachia *130*

M
milk bottles 80, *91*
milk churns *136*
misting flowerheads 9
molucella *122*
moss, Spanish *108*
muscari 113

N
narcissi 10, 114
  paperwhite 14, *136*
nerines *86*

O
oak *30*
oasis *56*
odd numbers in arrangements 10
orange kangaroo paw 114
orchids 114
  dendrobium *23*, *82*
  phalaeonopsis (moth orchids) *122*
  vanda *60*

P
pans, copper 80
pen pots *73*
peonies 13, 14, *21*, 34, *105*
peppercorns *108*
phytolacca berries *116*
pine 16, *29*
pinks 34
pomegranates *85*
poppy heads *49*
posies *105*
proteas *82*, *86*, *106*, *121*
pussy willow 34

R
ranunculus 113, *116*
rosehips 79, *86*

PICTURE CREDITS

Ryland Peters & Small and Jane Packer would like to thank the following home owners who so kindly allowed us to photograph their homes for this book, including:

Mark Homewood

Sue A'Court
www.suewilliamsacourt.co.uk

Jo Berryman
www.matrushka.co.uk
joanna@matrushka.co.uk

Chaucer Road/Light Locations
www.lightlocations.co.uk

Victoria Davar and Shane Meredith
of Maison Artefact
Maison Artefact
273 Lillie Road
London SW6 7LL
www.maisonartefact.com
mail@maisonartefact.com

Sarah Delaney
Sarah Delaney Design
www.sarahdelaneydesign.co.uk
020 7221 2010

Charlotte-Anne Fidler and Matthew Griffiths
www.airspaces.co.uk

ACKNOWLEDGMENTS

At the risk of repeating myself, this has been the hardest book I have created. Without the help of so many people it would not have happened at all. I am delighted that it has all come together and so grateful to everyone who has made it possible.

So, huge thanks to the following people: Catherine Gratwicke, so creative, patient and lovely. Lesley Dilcock for amazing styling; she always adds that little something extra to make a picture so special. Alison Starling for commissioning this book and having the faith that I would deliver. Leslie Harrington, who I have known for so long and who is forever helping with her creativity and patience. Annabel Morgan for her words – how can I thank her enough? She has helped me in so many ways, without her I think I would have gone crazy! Jess Walton for hunting down the wonderful locations. And Sonya Nathoo for her perfect layouts.

A special thank you to all of my team at Jane Packer, especially Susan, who has helped me so much over the years, and to Charlotte, for her endless hard work, making this book possible.

And finally thank you to my most cherished Gary, Rebby and Lola – what would I do without you?